I0427021

The Lazy Winner's Handbook

Discipline Yourself And Elevate Your Productivity Levels

Christopher V. Matthews

Contents

Introduction

It is possible that in a culture that places a high emphasis on laborious effort and productivity, laziness is seen as a negative characteristic. What would happen, however, if we were to rethink this notion and consider laziness to be a strategy?

strategy for maximising productivity and achieving the greatest possible results, rather than a sign of weakness? The art of sloth, which is a method of thinking that prioritises working more wisely above working harder, comes into play at this point in the process.

The art of idleness is not about being lazy or putting things off; rather, it is about making the most of one's time and resources to maximise one's productivity. Optimising processes, automating boring duties, and focusing on high-impact efforts that deliver significant results are all necessary steps in this process.

individuals may see idleness as a chance to free up time and energy for genuinely significant activities, such as personal growth, creative efforts, or just taking joy in life's simple pleasures. This is because idleness provides an opportunity for individuals to do these things.

It is necessary to make a mental change to adopt this attitude of laziness. This involves shifting away from the notion that being busy is a badge of honour and toward an appreciation of straightforwardness and effectiveness.

It involves going against the grain and challenging the status quo in an attempt to discover ways to carry out tasks that are more productive and suitable for the situation at hand. People can work smarter, not harder when they master the art of being lazy. This is because they can recognize inefficiencies and come up with inventive remedies for them.

During the subsequent analysis of the art of laziness, we will take a look at a variety of strategies and techniques that have the potential to aid individuals in cultivating this character trait in both their personal and professional lives.

We'll present practical tips on leveraging laziness as a tactical advantage in the fast-paced world of today, from time management tactics to automation technology. Together, let's explore the changing power of the art of laziness as we start on our expedition.

Chapter 1

Understanding Laziness

Laziness is defined as the inability to motivate oneself to complete a task while possessing the necessary skills. It might also mean that you're sluggish or slow-moving. Being lazy is a personal concept that may change depending on one's culture, social status, and personal beliefs.

Examining its origins and expressions: Laziness may take many different forms and have many different causes. Abuse or trauma, genetic predisposition, mental health conditions, chemical imbalances in the brain, environmental factors, boredom, fear of failing, low self-esteem, lack of goals, and procrastination are a few of these.

Feelings of depression, annoyance, guilt, or worthlessness, as well as decreased output, subpar performance, low energy, sleep problems, changes in eating, medical illnesses, and social disengagement, may all be indicators of laziness.

Acknowledging its impact on life both personally and professionally: Being lazy may have negative effects on one's life both personally and professionally.

It might have an impact on one's ability to meet goals, finish tasks, and maintain relationships. It could also be a factor in decreased well-being, satisfaction, and self-confidence. One's career, financial prospects, and physical and emotional well-being may all be negatively impacted by laziness.

Chapter 2

The Psychology of Laziness

Laziness is a common human trait that involves a lack of motivation or effort to perform a task or activity. Laziness can have various psychological causes and consequences, as well as cognitive and behavioural patterns that contribute to it. In this essay, I will briefly discuss some of the psychological theories behind laziness, the cognitive biases that enable it, and the behavioural outcomes of lazy thinking.

- ## Psychological Theories Behind Laziness

One psychological theory behind laziness is that it is a result of an instinct for idleness, which conserves energy and resources for survival. According to this theory, laziness is an adaptive response to an environment that does not require much activity or challenge. However, this theory does not explain why some people are more lazy than others, or why laziness can persist even in stimulating or demanding situations.

Another psychological theory behind laziness is that it is a form of self-sabotage, which stems from a fear of success or failure. According to this theory, laziness is a way of avoiding the potential risks or responsibilities that come with achieving one's goals or fulfilling one's expectations.

Some people may fear success because they think they do not deserve it, or because they worry about losing it or disappointing others. Some people may fear failure because they think it will damage their self-esteem, or because they dread the consequences or criticism. By being lazy, they can rationalise their lack of achievement or progress as a result of external factors, rather than their abilities or efforts.

• Cognitive Biases and Laziness

Cognitive biases are mental shortcuts or errors that influence our thinking and decision-making. Cognitive biases can enable or reinforce laziness by making us avoid or minimise the cognitive effort required to process information or perform a task. Some of the cognitive biases that are related to laziness are:

1. Confirmation bias: the tendency to seek, interpret, and remember information that confirms our existing beliefs or preferences, and to ignore or reject information that contradicts

them. Confirmation bias can make us lazy by making us selective and biassed in our information processing, and by reducing our curiosity and openness to new or alternative perspectives.

2. Availability heuristic: the tendency to judge the frequency or probability of an event based on how easily we can recall or imagine examples of it. Availability heuristics can make us lazy by making us rely on our memory or intuition, rather than on more objective or reliable sources of information, and by making us overestimate or underestimate the likelihood or importance of certain outcomes.

3. Sunk cost fallacy: the tendency to continue investing in a course of action or a decision, even if it is no longer beneficial or rational, because

of the time, money, or effort that has already been invested in it. Sunk cost fallacy can make us lazy by making us stick to our previous choices or commitments, rather than re-evaluating them or changing them, and by making us waste our resources or miss out on better opportunities.

- ## Behavioral Outcomes of Lazy Thinking

Lazy thinking can lead to various behavioural outcomes that can affect our productivity, performance, or well-being. Some of the behavioural outcomes of lazy thinking are:

1. Procrastination: the act of delaying or postponing a task or a decision, often in favour of more enjoyable or less demanding activities. Procrastination can be a result of lazy thinking, as we may avoid or put off a task that

requires cognitive effort, or that causes us anxiety or boredom.

2. Procrastination can also be a cause of lazy thinking, as we may lose focus or motivation, or miss deadlines or opportunities, as a result of our procrastination.

3. Indecision: the inability or unwillingness to make a decision or a choice, often due to a lack of information, confidence, or clarity.

4. Indecision can be a result of lazy thinking, as we may avoid or postpone a decision that requires cognitive effort, or that involves uncertainty or trade-offs. Indecision can also be a cause of lazy thinking, as we may remain stuck or passive, or rely on others or chance, as a result of our indecision.

5. Apathy: the lack of interest, enthusiasm, or concern for anything or anyone. Apathy can be a result of lazy thinking, as we may lose or suppress our emotions, values, or goals, or become indifferent or detached from our environment or ourselves.

Apathy can also be a cause of lazy thinking, as we may lack the motivation or energy to engage or participate in anything or anyone, or to change or improve our situation or ourselves.

Chapter 3

Setting Clear Goals

Setting clear objectives is a critical step to attaining success in every aspect of life. Goals help you concentrate your attention, encourage you to take action and assess your progress. However, not all objectives are created equal. Some objectives are more helpful than others in helping you overcome lethargy and accomplish your intended results.

One of the most popular and beneficial frameworks for defining goals is the SMART goal framework. SMART stands for Specific, Measurable, Achievable, Relevant, and

Time-bound. These factors help you set objectives that are clear, practical, and relevant.

1. particular: A particular aim addresses the questions of who, what, where, when, why, and how. For example, instead of declaring "I want to learn a new skill", a particular goal might be "I want to learn how to play the guitar by taking online lessons twice a week for six months".

2. Measurable: A measurable aim offers a mechanism for measuring your progress and assessing your performance. For example, instead of stating "I want to improve my health", a quantifiable goal might be "I want to lower my blood pressure by 10 points and lose 5 kilograms in three months by exercising for 30 minutes every day and following a balanced diet".

3. attainable: An attainable aim is within your grasp and talents. It should push you, but not overwhelm you. For example, instead of announcing "I want to be a millionaire", a feasible goal might be "I want to increase my income by 10% this year by taking on more projects and negotiating better rates with my clients".

4. Relevant: A relevant objective resonates with your particular beliefs and goals. It should be something that you care about and that matters to you. For example, instead of expressing "I want to travel the world", a relevant aim might be "I want to visit Japan next year because I love Japanese culture and want to learn more about it".

5. Time-bound: A time-bound aim has a particular deadline or period. This helps you establish a feeling of urgency and prioritise your efforts. For example, instead of declaring "I want to write a book", a time-bound goal might be "I want to write a 50,000-word novel by the end of November by writing 1,667 words every day".

By utilising the SMART goal structure, you may develop objectives that are more likely to help you overcome lethargy and accomplish your intended outcomes. You may also employ positive self-talk, reward yourself for your accomplishments, and seek encouragement from others to keep motivated and focused on your objectives.

Chapter 4

Creating Action Plans

An action plan is a detailed roadmap of the necessary steps you need to take to accomplish a specific goal or objective. It helps you break down a large goal into smaller, more manageable tasks, which makes the goal feel less overwhelming. To create an effective action plan, you can follow these steps:

1. Set SMART goals. SMART stands for Specific, Measurable, Achievable, Relevant, and Time-bound. A SMART goal is clear, realistic, and has a deadline. For example, instead of saying "I want to increase sales", you

could say "I want to increase sales by 20% within the next six months".

2. Create a list of actions. Identify the smaller tasks that need to be completed to achieve your goal. Break down complex tasks into subtasks to make them more manageable. For example, to increase sales, you could: improve your online presence, reach out to potential clients, and offer promotions.

3. Set a timeline. Assign realistic due dates for each task, and if needed, break them down into smaller milestones. A timeline will enable you to monitor your progress and stay on track. For example, you could set a deadline of October 15th for revamping your website design.

4. Designate resources. Determine what resources you need to complete each

task, such as money, time, people, or tools. Allocate these resources accordingly and ensure they are available when needed. For example, you could budget $500 for website design and hire John to do it.

5. Monitor the progress. Regularly review the tasks you've accomplished, and make note of the tasks that were challenging or required more time than anticipated. This self-assessment will help you improve your action plan and make necessary adjustments as you work towards your goal. For example, you could check your website analytics weekly and track new clients monthly.

Some useful skills that can help you with your action plan are:

1. Breaking down goals. Breaking down goals is the key to achieving major success. It involves identifying the major goal and defining specific, measurable objectives. Then, you can break down these objectives into smaller, actionable tasks. This technique helps you simplify complex goals, focus on the most important aspects, and avoid feeling overwhelmed.

2. Prioritising tasks effePrioritizingoritising tasks effectively means deciding which tasks are more important or urgent than others and doing them first. This skill helps you manage your time and resources better, reduce stress, and achieve your goals faster. Some methods to prioritise tasks are the

Eisenhower matrix, the ABCDE method, and the Pareto principle.

3. Time management techniques. Time management techniques are strategies to organise and use your time efficiently and productively. This skill helps you balance your work and personal life, meet deadlines, and avoid procrastination.

Some examples of time management techniques are the Pomodoro technique, the time-blocking method, and the SMART criteria.

Chapter 5

Overcoming Procrastination

Procrastination is the act of delaying or postponing an activity that has to be done. It may have significant implications on one's personal, academic, or professional life, such as increased stress, poor performance, and low self-esteem. Therefore, it is necessary to understand how to overcome procrastination and become more productive and effective.

One of the first stages to combat procrastination is to understand the factors that cause it.

Some frequent causes are:

- Fear of failure or success
- Perfectionism
- Lack of desire or interest
- Low self-confidence or self-efficacy
- Distractions or temptations
- Ambiguity or complexity of the task
- Poor time management or planning abilities

Once the triggers are recognized, one may employ several tactics to fight procrastination, such as:

- Setting specified, measurable, attainable, relevant, and time-bound (SMART) objectives
- Breaking down big or complicated jobs into smaller and easier subtasks
- Using incentives and penalties to push oneself
- Seeking social support or responsibility from others

- Eliminating or reducing distractions and temptations
- Creating a suitable atmosphere for work
- Using positive affirmations or self-talk
- Adopting a growth mindset and learning from errors

Another crucial strategy for overcoming procrastination is to generate momentum via minor triumphs. This suggests that one should start with the simplest or most fun work, or the one that has the greatest immediate value, and then go on to the next one.

In this manner, one may build a feeling of progress and success, which can enhance one's drive and confidence. Moreover, one may employ the Pomodoro approach, which entails working on a job for 25 minutes, followed by a 5-minute break, and continuing this cycle until the task is done.

This may allow one to stay concentrated and prevent burnout.

Chapter 6

Motivation Techniques

Motivation is the motivating force that helps us pursue our objectives and conquer problems. It may be impacted by both internal and external influences, such as our interests, values, rewards, feedback, and surroundings.

In this post, I will cover three motivation approaches that might help us reach our personal and professional objectives: intrinsic vs. extrinsic motivation, identifying sources of inspiration, and fostering a development mindset.

- Intrinsic vs. Extrinsic Motivation

Intrinsic motivation is the motivation that comes from inside us, such as our curiosity, passion, or delight. Extrinsic motivation is the incentive that originates from outside sources, such as money, grades, praise, or recognition. Both sorts of motivation may be successful, depending on the context and the person. However, research has found that intrinsic motivation tends to be more persistent and rewarding since it is based on our own beliefs and interests, rather than external incentives or demands.

Therefore, one motivation approach is to discover and pursue things that we find intrinsically compelling, such as hobbies, acquiring new skills, or volunteering for a cause. These activities may offer us a feeling of autonomy, competence, and purpose, which are crucial for our well-being and enjoyment. Moreover, we may also strive to improve our intrinsic motivation for things that we find less attractive, by finding methods to make them more significant, difficult, or entertaining. For example, we may establish our objectives, request feedback, reward ourselves, or gamify the process.

- Finding Sources of Inspiration

Another motivating strategy is to identify sources of inspiration that might stimulate our creativity and excitement. Inspiration may come from different sources, such as people, places, literature, music, art, or nature.

These sources may spark our creativity, extend our viewpoint, and fuel our enthusiasm. Inspiration may also encourage us to take action, as we feel compelled to express ourselves, share our thoughts, or contribute to something higher than ourselves.

Therefore, one motivating strategy is to expose oneself to different and exciting sources of inspiration, such as reading books, listening to podcasts, watching documentaries, visiting museums, or travelling to new areas.

These sources may supply us with fresh ideas, information, and experiences, which can expand our thinking and creativity. Moreover, we might also seek inspiration from others who inspire us, such as role models, mentors, classmates, or friends. These folks may give us direction, support, feedback, or cooperation, which can boost our learning and performance.

- Cultivating a Growth Mindset

A third motivating strategy is to establish a growth mindset, which is the concept that our talents and intellect can be increased through work and study. A growth mentality contrasts with a fixed mindset, which is the assumption that our talents and intellect are fixed and cannot be improved. Research has shown that adopting a growth mindset may enhance our motivation since it makes us more resilient, optimistic, and interested. A growth mindset also pushes us to accept difficulties, seek criticism, learn from failures, and celebrate success.

Therefore, one motivating strategy is to develop a growth mindset, by altering the way we think and speak about ourselves and our skills. For example, we may replace negative thinking, such as "I can't do this" or "I'm not good enough", with optimistic ones, such as "I can learn this" or "I can improve".

We may also employ positive language, such as "I'm working on this" or "I'm getting better". Furthermore, we may also cultivate a growth mindset, by creating realistic and precise objectives, exploring learning opportunities, incorporating feedback, reflecting on our progress, and enjoying our triumphs.

Chapter 7

Building Discipline

Building discipline is a core part of overcoming laziness and accomplishing one's objectives. It entails acquiring the capacity to constantly stick to a set of habits or routines that improve productivity and growth.

Developing self-discipline habits includes intentionally adopting actions that sustain discipline in everyday life. This may involve making particular timetables, generating to-do lists, and sticking to deadlines. By repeatedly adopting these behaviours, people learn to prioritise activities properly and avoid the temptation of procrastination.

Creating a suitable atmosphere for productivity is vital in fostering the development of discipline and self-discipline habits. This entails improving physical environments and removing distractions that may impair attention and productivity.

Designating a distinct workstation, arranging resources, and eliminating distractions may dramatically boost one's ability to focus and remain on target. Additionally, building a pleasant and encouraging culture may further inspire disciplined conduct by generating a feeling of purpose and desire.

Practising consistency and resilience is vital for retaining discipline in the face of obstacles and disappointments. Consistency means committing to disciplined acts regularly, even when motivation wanes or challenges emerge. This needs a steady determination to follow through with established chores and routines, regardless of external events. Resilience, on the other hand, is the capacity to bounce back from failures and continue in the pursuit of objectives.

By building a resilient attitude, people may overcome hurdles, learn from setbacks, and continue to grow on their quest towards overcoming lethargy and attaining success.

Chapter 8

Managing Energy Levels

Controlling our energy levels is essential to combating laziness since it directly affects our ability to engage in worthwhile activities. In this calculation, physical well-being is crucial. Maintaining good physical health has a positive effect on our energy levels in addition to improving overall wellbeing.

Maintaining energy levels throughout the day is mostly dependent on physical health, which includes frequent exercise, a balanced diet, and enough water. Exercise in particular improves mental clarity and alertness by boosting oxygen delivery to the brain and circulation. Exercise also reduces feelings of tiredness and inertia by releasing endorphins, neurotransmitters that are crucial for mood regulation.

Furthermore, nutrition is essential for providing the body with the fuel and nutrients it needs to operate properly. Minimising energy crashes and promoting stable blood sugar levels are two ways that a balanced diet full of fruits, vegetables, lean meats, and whole grains enhances sustained energy levels.

Another important factor that has a significant impact on energy and productivity is sleep hygiene. For mental clarity, emotional stability, and physical well-being, one must get enough sleep. Weak sleep hygiene may cause fatigue, headaches, and low motivation. It is characterised by irregular sleep schedules, short sleep durations, or poor sleep quality.

Maintaining good sleep hygiene requires practising relaxation techniques before bed, creating a peaceful sleep environment, and creating a regular sleep routine. In addition, it is important to make sleep a non-negotiable part of one's daily routine to combat fatigue and increase productivity.

Maintaining energy levels and combating lethargy need a lifestyle that includes both exercise and food. A nutritious diet and regular exercise provide the body with the resources it needs to function as intended throughout the day.

Exercise improves mood, increases mental clarity, and reduces sensations of weariness; on the other hand, a healthy diet feeds the body and prevents low energy. Stressing sleep hygiene also ensures proper rest, which is essential for mental clarity, emotional stability, and general productivity. Through these exercises, individuals may manage their energy levels and battle lethargy, ultimately leading to more effective achievement of their goals.

Chapter 9

Managing Energy Levels

Managing energy effectively is key to avoiding idleness and improving production. Physical well-being is vital to this process. Our bodies work at their best when they are well-fed and active, providing us with the energy we need to finish tasks rapidly.

This means adding exercise to our daily routines, which enhances physical fitness and activates the brain's synthesis of endorphins, which lower stress and encourage sentiments of wellness. In addition, sustaining energy levels throughout the day demands a nutritious diet. Eating a good, well-balanced meal feeds our bodies with the vitamins and minerals they need, decreasing energy slumps and increasing overall vitality. People may better manage their energy levels and battle tiredness by making physical health a priority via frequent exercise and a nutritious diet.

- The Value of Physical Well-Being in the Battle Against Laziness

Physical well-being is intimately tied to our abilities to fight indolence and maintain productivity. We are better able to overcome sentiments of lethargy and sluggishness when our bodies are in superb physical health.

Frequent exercise enhances cardiovascular health, muscular strength, and mood-regulating neurotransmitters, which all contribute to mental well-being.

Furthermore, exercise stimulates higher-quality sleep, which is vital for overall productivity. Sufficient sleep permits our bodies to rejuvenate and heal, boosting mental clarity and alertness in the waking state. Prioritising physical well-being via regular exercise and proper sleep helps individuals battle lethargy and enhance productivity.

- The Effects of Sleep Hygiene on Productivity

The habits and practices that promote peaceful sleep are referred to as sleep hygiene, and they have a substantial influence on our overall productivity. Insufficient sleep hygiene, which is characterised by unpredictable sleep patterns, using electronics soon before bed, and an uncomfortable sleeping area, may induce sleep problems like insomnia or fragmented sleep. As a consequence, individuals could feel lethargic during the day owing to weariness, problems with concentration, and a loss in willingness to perform duties. On the other side, following great sleep hygiene routines may boost the quality of your sleep and promote optimum productivity. These practices include providing a comfortable sleeping environment, keeping to a regular sleep schedule, and avoiding stimulants immediately before bed.

Better cognitive function, a longer attention span, and enhanced decision-making abilities are all helped by obtaining adequate sleep, which ultimately decreases the possibility of falling into lethargy when you're awake. Making proper sleep hygiene a priority can help individuals become more productive and feel better overall.

Chapter 10

Overcoming Perfectionism

Perfectionism, while generally seen as a beneficial characteristic, may become a hindrance when it leads to unachievable standards and excessive self-criticism. Understanding the challenges of perfectionism is crucial in overcoming its adverse implications.

Perfectionists tend to develop impossibly high standards for themselves, leading to constant unhappiness and fear of failure. This anxiety could inhibit people from taking action or completing things because they are always striving for flawlessness.

Moreover, perfectionism may strain relationships and limit collaboration, as the focus moves from progress to impossible perfection. To overcome perfectionism, individuals must learn to value imperfection and regard errors as opportunities for improvement.

- Understanding the Pitfalls of Perfectionism

Perfectionism may manifest in numerous forms, including procrastination, avoidance of difficulties, and excessive self-criticism. Perfectionists usually endure enormous worry and fear of failure, as they believe that any error reflects badly on their worth as humans.

This attitude may lead to a cycle of perfectionism where individuals feel imprisoned in a never-ending yearning for flawlessness. Furthermore, perfectionism may limit creativity and innovation, as individuals are afraid to take risks or explore new ideas for fear of falling short of their high standards. Recognizing these misconceptions is the first step towards overcoming perfectionism and developing a healthy attitude to productivity and personal growth.

- Embracing Imperfection and Learning from Failures

Embracing imperfection demands moving the focus from seeking perfection to making progress and learning from setbacks. Failure is not seen as a reflection of personal worth but rather as a potential for growth and self-improvement.

By reframing failures as helpful learning experiences, individuals may build resilience and adaptability in the face of hurdles. Embracing imperfection also implies letting go of the urge for external approval and loving oneself completely, embracing flaws and weaknesses. This shift in perspective supports a more positive and constructive approach to goal-setting and accomplishment, where progress is treasured over perfection.

- Setting Realistic Standards and Expectations

Setting realistic standards and expectations requires finding a balance between striving for excellence and recognizing boundaries. Rather than aiming for perfection, individuals should focus on setting appropriate aims that correspond with their abilities and resources. This means breaking down enormous tasks into smaller, doable actions and applauding progress along the way.

Setting realistic expectations also requires being adaptable and responsive to changing events, as perfection is usually elusive and context-dependent. By defining fair targets and acknowledging progress, individuals may preserve motivation and avoid the pitfalls of perfectionism.

Chapter 11

Seeking Support and Accountability

Although it's often presented as a positive quality, perfectionism may have negative impacts on one's productivity and general well-being. To counteract the detrimental effects of perfectionism, one must be aware of its traps.

Perfectionists often hold themselves to very high standards, which may lead to ongoing stress, worry, and a fear of failing. Because of the unreasonable notion that anything less than perfection is acceptable, this dread may paralyse people, stopping them from acting or finishing activities. Furthermore, perfectionism might prevent people from being creative or innovative because they concentrate too much on not making errors instead of taking chances and trying new things.

- Recognizing the Dangers of Perfectionism

Fear of criticism and a deep-seated desire for approval are the core causes of perfectionism. Perfectionists often equate their value to their accomplishments, which creates an endless loop of setting impossible goals and being disappointed when those goals are not reached.

This pattern feeds self-doubt and feelings of inadequacy, producing a vicious cycle that may be hard to escape. Furthermore, perfectionists often adopt an all-or-nothing mindset, seeing results as either flawless or total failures and failing to see the need for gradual improvement or learning from errors. This binary perspective strengthens an inflexible attitude that obstructs the advancement of the individual.

- Accepting Imperfections and Acquiring Knowledge from Errors

People who struggle with perfectionism need to learn to accept their flaws and see setbacks as chances for improvement. Accepting oneself and other people for who they are—flaws and all—and realising that perfection is an unachievable goal are all part of embracing imperfection. People can change their perspective from one of fear and avoidance to one of inquiry and resilience by reinterpreting mistakes as important teaching opportunities.

Accepting imperfection promotes an innovative and experimental culture where people are encouraged to take chances and try new things without worrying about failing or being judged. By changing their perspective, people may have a better connection with success and failure by realising that setbacks are not a reflection of their value but rather are necessary steps on the road to mastery and satisfaction.

Having Reasonable Expectations and Standards

Achieving lasting success and overcoming perfectionism requires setting reasonable expectations and standards. Realistic standards provide for a more balanced and doable approach to goal-setting by acknowledging the inherent constraints of time, money, and human capabilities.

People may lessen feelings of overload and feel more accomplished by establishing realistic objectives and dividing them into doable tasks. In addition, having reasonable expectations encourages self-acceptance and compassion as it acknowledges that errors and failures are inevitable aspects of learning. People may build a better attitude that values progress over perfection and embraces the process of personal growth and development by establishing reasonable standards and expectations.

Chapter 12

Seeking Support and Accountability

Fighting laziness and fostering personal improvement requires asking for help and taking responsibility for one's actions. It is necessary to surround oneself with people who encourage and propel progress toward goals to fully use social support networks.

This network might be made up of mentors, colleagues, friends, or relatives who provide guidance, encouragement, and helpful criticism. Through sharing goals and issues with this network of support, individuals may get vital information, perspective, and motivation to keep moving forward.

Organisations and partnerships dedicated to accountability provide a methodical approach to responsibility. This means forming bonds with others who share your goals and holding each other accountable for achievement. Whether formal or informal, accountability groups foster a sense of accountability and commitment to another's success.

Within these partnerships and groups, frequent check-ins, goal-setting meetings, and progress updates foster a sense of responsibility and motivation, reducing the likelihood of sluggishness settling in.

Alternatives to professional aid, including coaching and therapy, can provide specialised support and expertise in resolving underlying issues that cause laziness. Coaches provide tools, accountability structures, and strategies that are specifically designed to help clients overcome obstacles and reach their goals. In contrast, therapists focus on the deeper psychological issues that contribute to procrastination and indolence, providing targeted therapy to address underlying issues like anxiety, perfectionism, or low self-esteem.

These options for professional assistance provide an all-encompassing strategy for combating laziness and fostering personal development, complementing social support networks and accountability partnerships.

Conclusion

We have strolled through the numerous levels of expression of the art of idleness, explored its psychological roots, and disclosed the techniques to break free from its control. Our route has been distinguished by a detailed investigation of the variables creating lethargy and the proactive efforts to counteract them, from recognizing the fundamental causes to putting strategies into effect.

Through analysing the psychology of procrastination, developing self-control, regulating energy levels, and promoting mindfulness, we have given ourselves a toolset to efficiently navigate the complexities connected with laziness. To construct a road toward productivity and satisfaction, we have also underlined the significance of creating clear goals, seeking support structures, and nurturing an attitude of ongoing progress.

As we reach the closing of this presentation, let us not waver in our choice to fight the draw of laziness and live a life driven by purpose, tenacity, and unwavering resolution.